GANGS

TROUBLED

SOCIETY

GANGS

Renardo Barden

The Rourke Corporation, Inc.

The Rourke Corporation, Inc.
P.O. Box 3328, Vero Beach, FL 32964

Barden, Renardo.
     Gangs / by Renardo Barden.
         p. cm. — (Troubled society)
     Includes index.
     Summary: Discusses the phenomenon of gangs and how they reflect such social problems as poverty, racism, and drugs.
     ISBN 0-86593-073-2
     1. Gangs—United States—Juvenile literature. [1. Gangs.] I. Title. II. Series.
HV6434.U5B37   1990
364.1'06'0973—dc20   90-37515
                                               CIP
                                                AC

Series Editor: Gregory Lee
Editors: Elizabeth Sirimarco, Marguerite Aronowitz
Book design and production: The Creative Spark,
   Capistrano Beach, CA
Cover photograph: Robert Winslow/TomStack & Associates
Lyrics to "COLORS" (Ice T, Afrika Islam) Copyright 1988 COLGEMS-EMI MUSIC INC. & RHYME SYNDICATE MUSIC. All rights controlled and administered by COLGEMS-EMI MUSIC INC. All Rights Reserved. International Copyright Secured. Used by Permission.

GANGS

Contents

ONE

A TRAGEDY AND A COURTING IN

Not long ago, Gayle Thomas Kary, the mother of three young boys, experienced financial problems. She lived with her three sons in Long Beach, California, where there were youth centers and recreational programs. Her sons were good at sports and enjoyed the neighborhood centers. Unfortunately, she needed a cheaper place to live. Gayle Kary had to move to a house that her family owned in South Central Los Angeles.

Living was cheaper there, but less pleasant. The streets were alive with gang activity. The area was known for drug-dealing and, worse, for drive-by shootings. The neighborhood was home to different "sets" or chapters of the two most famous gangs on the west coast: the Crips and the Bloods.

One day Gayle Kary found her 13-year-old son Jamee cutting up a bar of soap. In small chunks, the white soap resembled crack cocaine, a drug being sold by gang members. Apparently Jamee was planning to fool a cocaine buyer by trying to sell him the crumbled soap. His mother was very upset. She arranged to send Jamee to stay with his father in Louisiana. She hoped that in Lousiana Jamee would be far from street gangs and cocaine. But Jamee's father said he couldn't handle the boy, and sent him back to Los Angeles.

Before long, Jamee stole his mother's car. The police stopped him, but because it was his mother's car, they only gave him a ticket for a traffic violation and sent him home. Gayle was furious. She drove Jamee back down to the police station and demanded that the police arrest him so he would learn his lesson. But the police were busy dealing with other crimes, and could not be bothered to

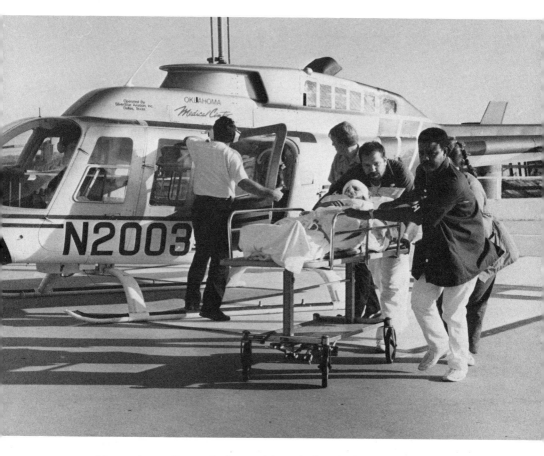

More and more the result of gang violence in America is another medical emergency, another gunshot victim, another funeral.

arrest her son.

Jamee was drawn more and more to life on the streets. He personally knew many gang members who were selling crack. They did not have to obey their parents, wash dishes, or help out around the house. They wore fine clothes, drove flashy cars, and always had money.

Soon Jamee began spending nights away from home with his gang-member friends. He became a member of a gang known as the Five Deuce

Broadway Crips. He sold drugs.

When Jamee was arrested for possession of cocaine with intent to sell, Gayle Kary was relieved. She hoped he would be confined to juvenile hall or placed in full-time custody. She hoped the authorities might help Jamee clean up his act. But the Los Angeles County Justice System put Jamee in juvenile hall for only a short time, then sent him to a youth camp. After five months Jamee was released.

After a few months back on the streets Jamee began to grow tired of gang life. He was on the run from police when he was away from home, and didn't always have a place to sleep. And he was often in danger from rival gang members. A probation officer suggested that Jamee apply to a special program. Getting into the program would mean that Jamee could live away from home, get off the streets of South Central L.A. and get away from gang life. Jamee said he'd give it a try.

Jamee was accepted, and seemed to do well in the program. After a short time he was allowed to spend a weekend at home with his family. On September 10, 1988—a Saturday evening during his weekend leave—Jamee asked his mother if he could go out with his friends for pizza.

Jamee hadn't been active as a gang member for many months. But a carload of Bloods, a rival gang, saw Jamee walking along the street and slowed down. Perhaps they recognized him or wanted to know what gang he belonged to. After a nasty exchange of words, the Bloods stopped their car and got out. Jamee turned to run, but he didn't make it. He was shot through the face. In a few minutes, he died.

For two years Gayle Kary had scolded her son, talked with police, sent Jamee to live with his father, and done everything she could think of to prevent something like this from happening. Nothing quite worked. Even though Jamee had finally decided to leave gang life behind him, the Bloods wouldn't let him. They shot him down because they believed that "once a Crip, always a Crip."

For too many young people, belonging to a gang is the most important thing in their lives. To understand this attitude requires some knowledge of this lifestyle as it is lived by thousands of youths in the United States.

Shadow Gets "Courted-In"

Not long ago, 30 members of a girls' gang took a young member-to-be known as Shadow behind some rusted cars in a junkyard. There, three members named Giggles, Shygirl and Rascal, removed their jewelry and wrapped their hands in scarves and bandanas. Then, while the gang counted slowly and loudly to 13, the three girls beat Shadow with their protected hands. When it was over, Shadow had messed-up hair, smudged lipstick, and a bloody nose. This was Shadow's "courting in." It was an initiation, an ordeal that meant Shadow was now a member of an L.A. street gang called the Tiny Diablas. Diablas is a Spanish term meaning "she devils." Diablas gang members are Latino; that is, they speak Spanish and are the children of Latino parents. Their "turf" is the Watts neighborhood in South Central Los Angeles.

Shadow was not badly beaten when she was courted-in, but if ever she wants out, or if members

The Ching-a-Lings, a female gang in New York City.

think she is no longer "down for the neighborhood," she can be "courted-out." In a court-out, there is no time limit to the beating she can receive.

There are about 30 Diablas between 14 and 18 years of age in South Central Los Angeles today. Many Diablas are girlfriends of the Grape Street Watts gang members. Some of their boyfriends are in jail for a variety of crimes. Their "homeboys" own and often carry guns, but they don't want the Diablas to have guns. Nevertheless, the Diablas have decided to take up a collection among themselves to buy guns anyway.

Although only misfortune can come of their owning guns, it is unusual when female gang members decide to acquire them. Studies show that girls' gangs are not as violent as boys' gangs. What is perhaps more interesting is that the Diablas are trying to show their independence from their homeboys' gang. Most of the time, Tiny Diablas gang members do just what their "homeboys" tell them to do.

Although girl gang members do not often participate in drive-by shootings or sell drugs on street corners, they are in danger because of their involvement with their homeboys. Many people who are killed in street shootings are innocent people who happen to be in the line of fire. More than a few victims have been girl gang members.

So what is the attraction of gang life? Why did Shadow allow herself to be beaten so she could become a gang member? What is it about gang life that attracted Jamee Kary? What is a gang, and what creates it? Do all gang members use drugs? Can gangs be done away with? These are just some of the questions we'll consider in this book. First, it's important to understand what a gang is, and what it is not.

What Is A Gang?

To an outsider, any group of loud teenagers in baseball caps and rolled-up jeans might look like a gang. Young people who talk loudly or dress in striking ways, or anyone who hangs out on street corners listening to rap music may look like a gang member. But exactly what are the differences between groups of friends and gang members?

According to the California Council on Criminal Justice, a gang is "a group of people who interact at a high rate among themselves to the exclusion of other groups. A gang has a group name, claims a neighborhood or other territory, and engages in criminal or other antisocial behavior on a regular basis."

The first part of the definition is not particularly helpful since it might just as well describe people at a country club, boys who skateboard in a mall parking lot, high school ski club members, or fans lined up for a rock concert.

The second part, however, assumes that the group is serious enough about itself to take a name. It assumes that the gang is involved in a struggle for territory. And perhaps—most importantly—it states that gangs engage in criminal or antisocial activities. Finally, the definition mentions criminal and antisocial behaviors as two separate activities.

A crime is an illegal activity expressly forbidden by law. Selling drugs, carrying a gun without a license, shooting people, or stealing money—these are crimes. Antisocial behavior is activity that disregards the rights of others. It may or may not be illegal. For

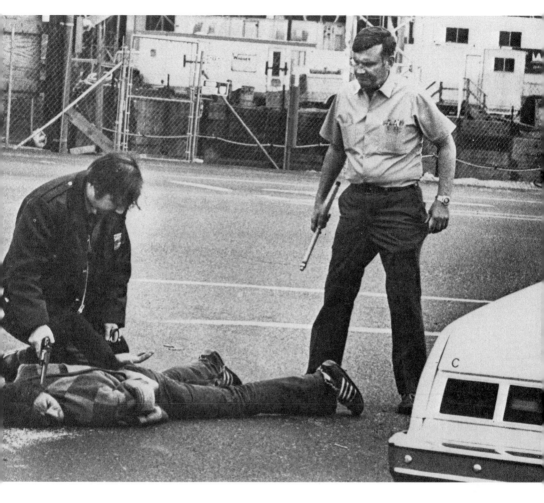

Gangs are no longer just a problem for America's largest cities, such as New York or L.A. Gangs and the violence they commit have become prominent in seemingly placid cities such as Portland, Oregon.

example, it may or may not be illegal to light a firecracker on a bus. Lighting a firecracker is certainly antisocial since it makes an unpleasant bang and gives off a foul odor. But it can also be dangerous to others (and fireworks of any kind are illegal in many communities). Smoking a cigar in a closed room, spitting in public, or playing loud music in a public place —all might be regarded as antisocial acts.

By themselves, definitions don't really help us understand how a gang gets to be involved in antisocial or criminal behavior, or why people join gangs in the first place. Some scholars have made special efforts to understand the appeal of gangs to individuals. The following discussion considers some of their ideas.

An Old Problem

Frederic M. Thrasher was a scholar connected with the University of Chicago in the 1920s. His 1927 book, The Gang, argued that gangs were often training grounds for adult criminals. Thrasher was the first to question the effectiveness of punishing youthful criminals with prison sentences. He said this was not effective for changing gang member behavior because gang members outside prison often admired convicts.

Another early scholar observed that gangs offered their members rewards that couldn't be earned by the individuals outside the gang. Gangs provided members with acceptance, status, achievement, excitement, and money.

In the 1950s, Albert K. Cohen, a famous social scientist, argued that American society placed too much value on money and the things that money could buy. He said that American society offered high self-esteem to those who could easily acquire money and material things. Cohen claimed that gang members who stole cars were simply trying to achieve the social status enjoyed by those who had jobs or access to their parents' cars.

Some experts believe that gangs are a regular part of lower class life in America. Lower class culture, according to Walter Miller, is marked by households headed by mothers only. Their children are not always carefully supervised. Children from these families tend to be poor. They often live in high-crime areas and become streetwise at an early age. Since they lack money, they learn to provide their own excitement. Miller said that gang life appeals mainly to adolescents, males who live in cities, equipped only for simple jobs. Miller believed that the goals of individual gang members are like the goals of non-gang members. He claimed that theft would be less a problem if there were more efforts made to improve the lives of poor young males who live in cities.

Miller's ideas have been criticized. Some thinkers have said that the conditions Miller described do not automatically lead to delinquency or gang behavior. Others have said that Miller is wrong to blame the American way of life for the decisions of young males to engage in criminal behavior. Poverty does not force people to break the law. However, it might encourage them to do so.

Cohen and Miller might almost have been writing in advance about the Crips and Bloods, two street gangs that originated in Southern California. These two street gangs, who have become active in more than a dozen states, fit the models established by Cohen and Miller. A typical member of these gangs is born in a poor neighborhood, lives in a household headed by his mother and, lacking money, soon learns to provide his own excitement. However dangerous, selling drugs and trying not to be caught by

Graffiti is a familiar way for gangs to mark their turf.
Subways and other public places throughout the U.S. are often marred by the symbols, slang and obscenities spray painted on buildings by gang members.

police or ripped off by dealers or buyers provides excitement. Since it brings in money, drug dealing also promises an escape from poverty.

TWO

GANGS, POVERTY AND RACISM

Although being poor by itself does not cause gang activity, there is evidence that poverty encourages young people to believe that gangs can provide the road to a better life. Poverty means going without important things. But for some people, the worst thing about being poor is having to ask and depend on other people for help. Prosperity can mean paying your own way. Poor but proud people are often drawn to gang life because by selling drugs they can get money and not have to ask others for help. For many, this benefit alone is more important than the things money can buy.

Looking south to the beautiful Caribbean, American and European tourists often vacation on the island of Jamaica. Jamaica has pristine beaches, a warm ocean to swim and scuba in, and first class hotels. Most people think of Jamaica as a happy place where reggae music comes from. Visitors see it as a place to relax and have fun. But many who live there, however, know differently.

Tourists rarely venture into the shantytowns where Jamaicans live crowded together in small huts built from wood and scrap. In these shantytowns, one outdoor basin may serve as the entire laundry facility for 1,000 people. As many as 100 people may share a single outhouse. Here poverty, prostitution, and robbery are a way of life. Unemployment can run as high as 95 percent. In these overcrowded ghettos, where many never learn to read and write, people must compete with one another for enough to eat. Lacking jobs, many young men spend their time smoking marijuana and drinking cheap beer. Poor Jamaicans see the rich lounging around the luxuri-

The oppressive poverty of some urban areas (such as the South Bronx)
breed youngsters who have no hope for a better life. Therefore,
joining a gang seems a logical way to fight for survival in a mean world.

ous hotels, throwing away food that people in the ghettos can't even afford, and enjoying luxuries the poor will never have.

So is it any wonder that some young Jamaicans have found a way out of this crushing poverty? They smuggle and deal drugs, especially marijuana and cocaine. If they make it to the United States, these same Jamaicans band together in gangs called "posses." Law enforcement officials believe as many as

10,000 native-born Jamaicans are involved in the United States drug trade today.

When these drug dealers return to visit Jamaica from their new homes in the United States, they wear expensive clothes and gold jewelry. They rent expensive cars. They have become what the Jamaicans call "dons," or drug dealers. It is easy to see why these dealers are often admired by younger Jamaican men and boys. As you might guess, some of these admirers also find a way to come to the United States.

Not long ago, police and federal agents arrested nearly 400 suspected members of drug-dealing Jamaican gangs in Houston, Miami, New York City and other large cities. They were not just dealing drugs, however. Police said these young men and women from the ghettos of Jamaica were wanted for over 1,400 drug-related murders since January 1985. They were also wanted in connection with kidnappings, robberies, gun smuggling operations, and other criminal offenses.

Authorities have said that the Jamaican posses are as violent as any gang that has ever been active in this country. Members of a group known as the Shower Posse, for example, were accused of murdering five people in a Miami crack house. Among the five was a pregnant woman whose body was found in a praying position. Police believe she had begged for her life just before she was killed.

The Role Of Racism

Gang members are typically members of the same ethnic group, and they often band together as a reaction to racism. Fear and hatred of people of another race is called *xenophobia* (zeen-o-foe-bee-uh). Gang members themselves are inclined to be xenophobic. Sometimes the people who are victims of racism become racists themselves. For example, rap music, inspired in part by racial prejudice encountered by young African-Americans, often features lyrics that are deliberately offensive to Jews, Asians, and women.

Early in this century, most cities in the eastern United States were rigidly divided into ghettos. For example, Italian-Americans lived with other Italian-Americans, and were not welcome to live in Irish-American neighborhoods. The same prejudices were applied against Asians, Jews, African-Americans, and Latino peoples (not to mention Native-Americans, who were hidden away on reservations). In those days, xenophobia was a way of life in the United States.

Although no longer as widespread, racial prejudice is still very much an everyday experience for millions of Americans. Blacks and Latinos in particular still meet with racism when they leave their neighborhoods. In most communities, Asians—notably Vietnamese, Cambodians and Chinese—are victims of prejudice as well.

Gangs come from all races. Apart from the Jamaican posses, there are Asian gangs who bring in heroin from Thailand by way of Hong Kong. There are South American gangs who bring cocaine in from Colombia. There are street gangs open only to African-Americans who sell crack on city streets. Hawaiian and Filipino gangs often traffic in the new drug called "ice." Latino gangs dominate the culture of East Los Angeles; Cuban gangs are very active in Miami; Korean gangs extort money from Korean businesses in California; and white skinhead gangs practice racism

Intimidation, robbery and murder by roving bands of youths is not new. Americans have even made heroes of some well-known violent criminals. This man's death was mourned by many law-abiding citizens—his name was Jesse James.

in the communities of San Francisco and Portland, Oregon, among other places.

In days gone by, gangs were organized like ethnic armies. If an Italian boy was beaten up by Irish boys, a gang of Italians would go into an Irish neighborhood and beat up an Irish boy. Other gangs behaved similarly. In time, many people came to recognize that violence against members of other races and ethnic groups was wrong. This is not to say that racial violence has completely died out, but rather that fewer people today behave violently toward people of another color or ethnic background.

Today's gangs, however, are still suspicious of other races and ethnic groups. They may sell drugs to people of any color, but they usually share or compete for street-corner space with members of their own ethnic groups. Their enemies are typically gang members of the same background.

For example, with large sums of drug money at stake, the Crips and Bloods continuously wage war against one another, beating and murdering members of their own ethnic groups. The same is true of Latino gangs in Los Angeles. They do not usually drive down to South Central Los Angeles to shoot blacks or to West L.A. to shoot whites. They drive the streets of their own neighborhoods or *barrios* to shoot fellow Latinos, whose language, culture and poverty most nearly resemble their own.

While gang members like to think of themselves as having racial and ethnic pride, crime statistics show that members most often prey on their own people in their own neighborhoods. Sometimes gang members leave their neighborhoods on gang missions—only to seek revenge against other gang members. That was the case not long ago when the Crips and Bloods wandered into an affluent neighborhood in West Los Angeles. In fighting their own gun battle, they accidentally shot and killed a 27-year-old graphic artist named Karen Toshima.

Afterwards, critics of the press used Toshima's

death to accuse journalists and police of racism. An attractive Japanese-American with a good job, Toshima was cut down outside an expensive restaurant in a wealthy neighborhood. Critics said that the newspapers, television stations, and police were outraged by Toshima's death only because she was in a "safe," all-white neighborhood at the time she was shot. They said that the murder of a black child that occurred in a primarily black South Central Los Angeles neighborhood the week before had been ignored. Two weeks after Toshima's death, a middle-aged African-American woman was cut down by gang gunfire, but the press paid little attention to the killing. Alma Washington's death went all but unnoticed.

When television and the newspapers did not pay as much attention to the killing of Washington as they had to Toshima, critics said the press was racist. The silence of the media in Washington's case reinforced an ugly message: that the death of a successful young person in a white neighborhood was considered more important than the death of an African-American woman and child in a poor neighborhood already troubled by violence. To their killers, the deaths of Toshima and Washington were not racially motivated. Toshima and Washington were not killed by Crips and Bloods because of their ethnic origins, but to the people of the black community, racism was the end result.

Michael Fleager, a probation officer in Orange County, California, has observed gang life for a long time. He understands that racism is part of gang life. "The *chicano* gangs go back three generations and turf is their motivation. Black gangs turn money into power into drugs. Asian gangs are into it purely for profit. And skinheads are motivated by racism," he says.

Skinheads

Most gangs are motivated by the chance to earn profits from selling drugs, or by the need to protect themselves or their neighborhoods from better organized groups. Only a few small, thinly organized groups band together entirely to promote racial hatred. So-called "skinheads" fall into this category.

Skinheads take their name and style from some British working class gangs who existed in the 1970s. A shaved head is characteristic of the "hard, clean" style favored by skinheads or, as they call themselves, "skins."

Not all skins believe in the supremacy of the white race, but those that do are considered to be part of the fastest growing hate group in the nation.

"In general hate groups are declining," says Irwin Suall, of the Anti-Defamation League of B'nai B'rith in New York City. "But this [racist] wing is growing. And one of the most troubling things is that it consists almost entirely of young people ages 16 to 25."

How big a problem is white racism today? It's still a significant social problem, although fewer Americans are willing to join organizations that promote white supremacy. For example, membership in the 125-year-old Ku Klux Klan has reached an all-time low. The Klan is an all-white organization formed in the south after the Civil War. It was dedicated to making black people afraid for their lives. Sometimes its members hanged and burned blacks without reason. The Klan believed that blacks should be kept in socially inferior positions by making them too afraid to speak out for racial equality.

Although there are fewer militant white racists

A police officer removes three skinheads from a demonstration at Georgia's state capitol. In recent years, an alarming number of young people have become involved in white supremacy organizations.

than there were a few years ago, the surviving members of these groups are perhaps more extreme in their views than the members who have left. A few skinheads have joined the Klan, while others belong to the White Aryan Resistance Movement (or WAR).

Skinheads have appeared on the Oprah Winfrey and Geraldo Rivera TV shows, where they were given a chance to argue their racist views before a national television audience. Much of their talk was just that—`talk —intended to shock viewers and boost television ratings.

Sometimes, however, their hate-filled talk turns to tragedy. Tough talk turned bloody in Portland, Oregon, on November 13, 1988, when three local skinheads beat a 27-year-old man to death with a baseball bat.

Killed was Mulugeta Seraw, a native of Ethiopia. Following an evening spent with friends, Seraw was returning to his apartment in southeast Portland. A car filled with young white men stopped and jumped him as he stood with a couple of friends.

A few days later, Kyle Brewster, 19, Steven Rodney, 20, and 23-year-old "Ken Death," whose real name is Kenneth Mieske, were arrested and charged with murder. The three were members of a swastika-wearing, Hitler-admiring gang known as East Side White Pride. Each has since been convicted of participating in the beating that resulted in Seraw's death, and has been sentenced to prison.

Few gangs are interested in actions intended to demonstrate their supposed racial superiority. But millions of Americans—gang members and nonmembers alike—have developed a fondness for drugs. Many street gangs have taken it upon themselves to cater to the need for these illegal paths to pleasure.

THREE

GANGS AND DRUGS

In the 1960s, spurred on by widespread interest in experimentation, public attitudes toward marijuana and the drug known as LSD or "acid" began to change. The smoking of marijuana, while still illegal, became socially acceptable in many parts of American society. The psychedelic drug LSD was popularized by a psychologist at Harvard University named Timothy Leary, and by some popular poets and rock singers.

Still others turned to heroin, a stronger, highly addictive drug that comes from the opium poppy. But because doses of the drug are expensive and have to be injected with a hypodermic needle or syringe, heroin has never been as popular as marijuana or cocaine.

"It's simple," says one New York cop, explaining why street addicts have switched from heroin to crack. "Why pay $20 to $30 for a bag of heroin when you can get just as intense a high from a $5 vial of crack?"

Today the use of LSD and heroin have fallen off. Marijuana, though still sold and smoked by some gangs, is not the drug of choice. Today's most popular street drug is cocaine or, in some places, crack cocaine.

Cocaine

Cocaine is extracted from the leaves of coca bushes that grow in South American countries such as Peru and Bolivia. The country of Colombia is linked with the cocaine business not so much because the plant grows there, but because Colombia leads the rest of the world in processing and smuggling the drug into the United States.

Coca plants are stripped of their leaves several times a year. The leaves are treated with chemicals and

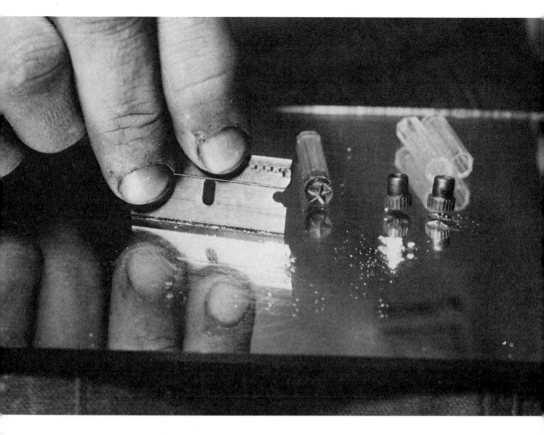

A vial of crack is cut with a razor blade to make it easier to inhale.
Street value of this dosage: $5.

eventually turned into a paste known as a base. Large laboratories continue to refine the base and add other chemicals. Eventually the lab produces an odorless white powder that looks like flakes or chunks of white soap.

Street dealers often dilute these flakes or chunks with other chemicals in order to have more cocaine to sell and make more money. Sometimes dealers mix cocaine with other drugs but just as often they mix it with corn starch, flour or talcum powder.

Cocaine can be snorted, injected or freebased

(smoked). Many users prefer to snort powdered cocaine by inhaling it through the nose. Most of the cocaine is then absorbed through nasal membranes. But some is wasted, never reaching the bloodstream. The absorbed amount of the drug reaches the brain in a few minutes and makes the user high for about 20 or 30 minutes.

Those who inject cocaine dissolve the powder with the help of water. The liquid mixture is drawn up into a syringe or hypodermic needle, then injected directly into a vein. This is a more efficient way of using cocaine, since all the cocaine is immediately carried to pleasure centers in the brain by the bloodstream. The drug takes effect immediately and brings on what is called a "rush."

Users of needles, however, are at risk more than those who snort cocaine. "Dirty" (unsterilized) needles can infect a user with a variety of diseases such as hepatitis and AIDS.

Cocaine can also be freebased, but first it must be treated with other materials. Cocaine users can make their own freebase or buy it already converted. Converted coke is known as "crack."

Crack Cocaine

In the United States crack is to street gangs what gasoline is to cars: it makes them operate and keeps them going. It is known as crack because of the sound made when the drug burns.

Crack is made by mixing cocaine with baking soda and water. When processed, the cocaine turns into little rock-like crystals known as "rocks." Crack is also known as "rock."

Users put the crushed chips into a tobacco or marijuana pipe or roll it in a cigarette, light the mixture, and smoke it. The drug reaches the brain immediately. It makes the user very high, but the high lasts for only a few minutes. Usually the user craves more right away. That is why crack is considered the most addictive drug now available.

By drug-user standards, crack is not particularly expensive. A dose can sell for as little as $5. On the west coast, crack is sold on a one-dose basis in a sealed plastic bag. On the east coast, a dose typically is sold in a clear vial. Although the price of a single dose is low, the crack user always wants to smoke more and more of the drug.

Cocaine, heroin and marijuana all come from plants that are grown around the world. That means drugs that come from plants can be limited by destroying the crops. With some drugs, however, there is no natural supply that can be limited because they do not need a warm, humid, environment in which to grow. Some drugs are made by people who have a knowledge of elementary chemistry.

Ice

With the numbers of crack-addicted young people and gang members growing every day, authorities on the west coast have recently begun to worry about a new drug. In Tokyo, Japan, they call this new drug *shabu*. In Seoul, Korea, it is known as *hiroppon*. In Hawaii and on the West Coast of the United States where it is just beginning to appear, they call it "ice" because it looks like ice crystals.

A highly potent form of the drug methedrine, ice was first made in Japan about a hundred years ago. During World War II, it was used by the Japanese army to produce a heightened sense of well-being and artificial courage in battle. When it was banned in Japan in the 1950s, people began to produce and import it from nearby Korea. It has been estimated that more than 130,000 Koreans are addicted to ice.

More recently, Filipino gangs have been selling the drug in Hawaii, and federal agents have been pursuing a Korean gang that has been selling it in the United States.

Ice gives its users enormous amounts of energy, causing them to stay awake for days at a time. For that reason, it is considered a "party" drug. It is also cheap. A small bag—called a paper—costs about $50, and will keep a dedicated user high for up to a week at a time.

Authorities are worried that even if they are finally able to dramatically reduce the amount of cocaine imported into the United States, ice will allow gang members to go on dealing drugs at a profit.

But as of now, drugs show no sign of becoming scarce. And gangs, many of them armed with the latest and most expensive assault weapons, car phones and beepers, have shown themselves more than able to keep up with their customers.

It's Money That Matters

In the old days before drugs became widely popular, many gang members struggled to escape the neighborhood and eventually left gang life behind. They went on to have jobs, marriages and families. But those days are largely gone.

For one thing, fast food restaurants, grocery stores and other businesses that hire young people don't like to open new outlets in troubled, gang-infested neighborhoods. So there are fewer unskilled jobs available in areas dominated by gangs. There is also less money available overall for on-the-job training, and fewer semi-skilled jobs that pay a living wage.

Influenced by the limited world they see on television, many young people believe it is better to not work hard at anything. The sports pages and music video channels are filled with stories of people who make huge amounts of money for doing next to nothing. Young people aspire to be very rich by being very famous. Television fosters a false idea about how easy it is to become a star.

Even if there were jobs available in gang neighborhoods, few gang members would probably want them. Once a young drug dealer has become accustomed to the so-called easy money of drug dealing, he's not too likely to settle down and work for minimum wage.

"In school," says Kevin Rogers, a Los Angeles Police Department detective, "these kids are told to work real hard and study and get a job at Burger King by becoming manager and at 21 they'll have a house and a mortgage, and they'll laugh. They'll tell you they can make more money and have better clothes than you right now [by] standing out there on the street corner selling rock [crack cocaine]."

Things are no different on the east coast when it comes to the money-making opportunities of drug dealing. "Crack is a cottage industry," says a narcotics prosecutor in New York named Sterling Johnson, Jr. "Anybody who's got a little coke, bicarbonate of soda, and some balls thinks they can be an entrepreneur now. With the way it's made, if you have $20,000

A "crack house"—in this case, a boarded-up brownstone dwelling—where drug customers gather to buy and smoke crack off the street.

worth of coke, you sell $80,000 worth of crack. There's a new generation of kids selling out there that we don't even know about. A lot of them in their late teens or early 20s....They're reckless and they don't care about the future. They do their talking with guns."

Selling and using crack is almost always connected with murder and violence. But Terry Williams, a scholar at the City University of New York (CUNY), decided to call attention to the ways that dealing drugs resembles starting and operating a profitable business. He wrote and published Cocaine Kids, a study that focuses on young people in New York who dealt cocaine for several years.

"Money and drugs are the obvious immediate rewards," says Williams. "But there's another strong motivating force, and that is the desire to show family and friends that they can succeed at something.... A kid who can routinely handle money, control personal use of cocaine, deal with buyers and control a weapon may make it out of the streets and into the elite world of the superdealer."

Williams believes that New York state's so-called Rockefeller Law, which mandates a prison sentence for any drug dealer over the age of 18, has driven some young people in a different direction. His study tracks a group of teenaged cocaine dealers over a period of four years in Queens, New York.

One of the dealers was a student at CUNY and used money made dealing to help him graduate from college. Another dealer saved enough to start a legal business in Florida. Another is learning to be a cook. One was wounded by a gun-toting dealer and is no longer dealing drugs. Only one of Williams' subjects was still dealing drugs after the four-year study.

The study suggests that not all people who set out to make money dealing drugs continue to deal until they become addicted; or until they are thrown in jail, killed, or seriously injured. Like gang members, Williams' subjects took risks and broke the law. They succeeded, at least partly. If all drug dealers are not killed or ruined by drugs, this helps explain why many gang members feel that dealing drugs may help them escape an unhappy life in the ghetto. Those who

Police who patrol gang-ridden neighborhoods face a constant threat to their safety.

choose to sell drugs gamble with something very important: their lives. Yet those who have never known anything but poverty, and have never owned anything valuable to call their own, are bound to find the money to be made from drugs very tempting.

Robert Jones, a Detroit narcotics officer, sees another side of drug dealing. "Every day you go to a high school and you see new Mercedes and Jeeps and Cadillacs and Volvos. These cars belong to the kids, not the parents."

Police in California say that dealers too young to have a drivers' license hire their own drivers. Others simply add driving without a license to their long list of criminal offenses.

Witness the case of a 12-year-old crack dealer

named Frog. He is a member of the Crips who lives in East L.A. and earns $200 a week selling crack. Frog bragged to a reporter that he used his drug money to rent a Nissan on weekends. At the time he couldn't even drive a stick shift car. At 4'10", he couldn't see over the windshield. But lack of height or a valid driver's license didn't stop him from experiencing the kinds of driving pleasures many adults can't afford.

Los Angeles probation officer John Copley says that underaged drivers who buy expensive cars take a particular risk. "Whenever they're in an accident they have to get out and run away," he says. "They paid cash for the cars, but they don't have driver's licenses or insurance. Look in the police tow yards in Central Los Angeles. They are full of new Trans Ams, Blazers, Cadillacs that have been in minor accidents and the drivers just got out and ran."

FOUR

GANGS AND PROHIBITION

In 1919 the United States passed a law prohibiting the sale, importing or drinking of alcoholic beverages. This was known as Prohibition. For nearly 15 years it was illegal to manufacture, buy, sell, or drink alcoholic beverages in the United States. Prohibition was introduced and supported by people who thought that life in America would be better without beer, wine, and other liquors. They believed that drinking was immoral and led to crime.

Most Americans, however, did not believe that occasional use of alcohol was wrong. They did not like the government telling them what they could and couldn't do. Many simply refused to give up their long-standing habit of drinking. Laws that people refuse to obey prove useless. They are worse than useless, because they make criminals out of otherwise good people.

The United States government employed a few federal agents to enforce prohibition. But before long it became clear that making prohibition work in America would require an army. Millions of Americans were willing to pay for illegal alcohol. To cater to their desires, smugglers known as "bootleggers" sneaked whiskey and other alcoholic drinks across the Canadian border. They used ships and boats to bring liquor up from the Caribbean or across the ocean. Some people made "bootleg" whiskey in their homes and sold it to regular patrons of "speakeasies." Speakeasies were illegal nightclubs that sold alcoholic beverages to patrons. Often cab drivers and even police-

Al Capone, the most powerful gangster in Chicago during prohibition. The gangs or "mobs" of the 1920s and '30s sold alcohol illegally for huge profits. They were the forerunner of today's gangs who thrive on illegal drug profits.

men could tell out-of-town visitors where to find the nearest speakeasy.

The worst thing about prohibition was that virtually anyone willing to take risks and murder rivals could make millions of dollars. By 1927, a small-time Chicago gangster named Al Capone had developed a $60 million business based on manufacturing, smuggling, and selling alcohol. In his private war against others who also wanted to bootleg liquor, he organized a gang of 1,000 men who "ran" Chicago. In the years 1926 and 1927, Capone's gangsters were responsible for about 130 murders—most of them connected to the illegal business of liquor.

Prohibition was repealed in 1933, and Americans were legally free to drink again. By then, however, most American cities had a "gang problem." Men and women who had become wealthy by disregarding the liquor laws now had "organized" crime to contend with. These "families" often shared areas of a city with rival groups. Sometimes they fought rivals in the streets. Sometimes they killed policemen. They hired skilled lawyers to defend them in court. When prohibition was over, they opened illegal gambling clubs and organized prostitution to make up for the loss of income from liquor. In time they began selling drugs.

Although most of these prohibition gangs were broken up by years of police work that cost Americans millions of dollars, their legacy of disregard for the law lives on. To some extent, so does their investment in crime. Gangs learned a fundamental truth of American society: there would always be customers willing to break the law for substances that would make them high.

Should Drugs Be Legalized?

"My mind is too sharp, my body is too precious to foul it with drugs," said Washington, D.C., Mayor Marion Barry not long ago. But even as he said those words, there were police and other authorities in Washington who thought that Barry was being false or hypocritical. He was the mayor of a city where there had been 480 homicides in 1989—many of them drug and gang related.

One day early in 1990, Mayor Barry attended a memorial service for a high school star athlete who was shot to death while walking in a drug-infested neighborhood. In the evening he went to a Washington motel, where he was arrested by police who said he had been using cocaine.

When the mayor of one of the country's largest and most drug-crippled cities is arrested for drug usage, the war on drugs is in serious trouble. Many experts in law, sociology, and medicine have begun to ask: Should drugs be legalized?

Those who support the legalization of drugs point to what happened during prohibition. The manufacture and sale of alcohol in the United States was forbidden, but people chose to ignore the law. Some compare efforts once made to force people to stop drinking to modern efforts to prevent people from using drugs. They argue that the laws against drug use have not been effective.

The case of Mayor Barry also illustrates a double-standard in American society. While drug users with money and prestige can afford expensive clinics to receive help with their drug problems, those without money are sent to prison or are required to wait

Motorcycle gangs used to be the most intimidating in American society
standards. Chains and "brass knuckles" have

months or years to get help with their addictions.
Before they can be helped, many of these people are
shot to death in the streets trying to buy cheap drugs.

There is, of course, widespread agreement that
drugs are generally bad for people's health. Those
favoring legalization argue that people now taking
drugs won't give them up. They argue that laws that
don't work and are unevenly enforced won't stop
future drug use. Some of these people believe that if
there were no laws that made users and sellers liable

during the 1950s and '60s. Now these aging bikers seem tame by today's
given way to semiautomatic weapons.

to arrest, illegal drugs would become readily available and therefore would become inexpensive. As a result, illegal, violent behavior to get drugs would not be necessary.

What might happen if drugs were legalized and taxed by the government? For one thing, taxes paid by drug sellers could be used to cure people who wanted to be free of drugs. Gangs like the Crips and Bloods would be unable to make huge profits selling illegal drugs.

Gang warfare and racial violence often go hand-in-hand.
These Miami police officers are armed in riot gear as a house goes up in flames behind them.

But many people, including President Bush and his drug chief William Bennett, strongly oppose the legalization argument. They say that drugs are much more destructive than alcohol, and that if drugs were legalized, more—rather than fewer—people would use them. This has not proven to be the case in some parts of Europe, however, where drug use is more tolerated and—in some cases—legal.

Those who favor a continuation and expansion of present drug policies say that if drugs were legalized, addicts would not be motivated to seek help. But perhaps the strongest argument against legalizing drugs is made by Bennett, who says that each year as many as 10,000 babies are born to drug-addicted mothers. Because they are nourished by their mothers' blood before birth, these babies are often born addicted. Many babies of drug-using mothers have severe health problems or are born dead. These babies, Bennett points out, do not choose to use drugs.

Bennett believes America will win the war on drugs. Others disagree. The one sure thing is that this argument will go on for a long time. Neither side of the legalization argument is willing to stop the debate.

FIVE

DEADLY RIVALS

Although there are street gangs in every city from coast to coast, Los Angeles seems to have more gang members than any other American city. Police estimate that there are between 60,000 and 70,000 gang members in Los Angeles County.

It is a shocking fact that between 1970 and 1987 nearly 3,000 people were killed by gangs in L.A. County. In addition, about 15,000 people were seriously injured. About 600 of the killed and injured were non-gang members and innocent bystanders.

In 1980, Mike Redmond, a Los Angeles gang member, was sitting with a friend and fellow gang member in the friend's front yard. As a car drove down the street, sounds of gunfire shattered the quiet of the neighborhood. When the car drove off, Redmond's 20-year-old friend was fatally wounded.

"They blew his brains out," Redmond said. "He died in my arms." The victim's mother ran out of the house, screaming, "Why couldn't it have been you?" Redmond had no answer for her. He knew it could easily have been him.

Before he left gang life, Redmond had served three years in prison and attended the funerals of six good friends. Now in his middle 30s, Redmond founded the Compton Crips when he was 13 years old. The Compton Crips, however, are only one among many "sets" of Crips. As of today there are hundreds of Crips sets.

Today, working as a street corner counselor for the Community Youth Gang Services in Los Angeles, Redmond knows he was one of the lucky ones. "I feel very bad," Redmond said, "because I'm one of the major [causes]

Another drive-by shooting. This Brooklyn man was murdered by three unidentified men as they passed him in a car.

of what's happening in Compton right now."

Many authorities believe the Crips were formed at Washington High School in South Los Angeles during the 1960s. As to the origins of the gang name, some people think the term "Crip" comes from a misspelling of the term kryptonite, the nonexistent mineral that could (according to comic book lore) kill Superman. Others insist that "crips" is a shortened form of "cripplers" —gang members who cripple. At one time, gang members claimed they punished their enemies by shooting them in the knees so they would never again be able to walk without limping.

Gang wars over territory and the market for crack cocaine have changed many aspects of gang life. So has the ownership of expensive cars and automatic and semiautomatic weapons. This is the era of the drive-by shooting, when gang members shoot to kill, in neighborhoods and on freeways, then drive away.

While the Crips emerged as a powerful gang in South Central Los Angeles in the early 1970s, other street gangs began to take the name Crip and add it to their own gang names. The Main Street gang became the Main Street Crips; the Rollin' 20s Gang became the Rollin' 20s Crips, and so on.

In some cases, however, neighborhood feuds and rivalries would not allow for the adoption of the name Crips. So other gang members took the name of "Bloods" and organized themselves into their own "sets" in order to survive the Crips' violence.

In the early days of the gangs, sets considered it wrong to attack members of another set. A Crip from one set would not shoot, knife, or start a fight with a Crip from another set. The same held true with Bloods.

Gradually, however, there were so many sets of Crips that they found themselves at war with others over "turf," or the control of a neighborhood. It's now generally agreed that contrary to earlier days, a Crip will kill a Crip, and a Blood will kill a Blood.

The Crips and Bloods originated in Los Angeles. But money from drug sales has provided members of both gangs with the means and desire to branch out. Members of both sets have recently been reported in

Seattle, Phoenix, Portland, Denver, San Diego, and even Chicago.

Showing Your Colors

Gang styles change from year to year and from season to season. A few items, however, seem fairly constant to the styles of the Crips and Bloods. Both gangs favor khaki slacks—the baggier, the better. They like wearing clean white T-shirts, thin belts, and bandanas stuffed in the back pocket of their slacks or worn around their heads. Tattoos are common, as are earrings. Hair is usually worn naturally or in elaborate braids called corn rows.

The Crips' color is blue, so Crips wear blue bandanas; the Bloods, whose color is red, favor red bandanas. Handkerchiefs, sweatshirts, sweaters, and the color and insignia on baseball caps (often worn backwards or sideways) signify gang loyalty, as do sneaker style and color of shoelaces.

Police and gang experts have noted a recent tendency to show colors less frequently. The reason is survival. More gang members are now carrying drugs or illegal weapons. To avoid being stopped by police, they often adopt a more conservative style of dress. Also, with the rising tide of drive-by shootings, gang members are less likely to show their colors without a good reason.

Outsiders and copycats try to dress like gang members. For example, rappers often adopt gang styles, use gang terms, and become successful doing it. Unfortunately, judging from other events, some imitators—probably not rappers—have been putting themselves in danger.

COLORS

A rap from the motion picture "Colors,"
a movie about L.A. gangs.

Colors
I am a nightmare walkin', psychopath-talkin'
King of my jungle just a gangster stalkin'
Livin' life like a firecracker—quick is my fuse
Been dead as a def back the colors I choose
Red or blue cuz a blood, it just don't matter
Sucker die for your life when my shotgun scatters
The gangs of L.A. will never die…just multiply.

Colors
You don't know me—fool!
You disown me?—cool!
I don't need your assistance, social persistance
Any problem I got I just put my fist in
My life is violent, but violent is life
Peace is a dream—reality is a knife!
My colors my honor, my colors my all
With my colors upon me one soldier stand tall
Tell me—what have you left me, what have I got?
Last night in cold blood a young brother got shot
My homeboy got jack, my mother's on crack
My sister can't work cuz her arms show tracks
Madness, insanity, livin' profanity
Then some punk claimin' they understandin' me?
Gimme a break! What world do you live in?
Death is my set—guess my religion!

Colors
My pants are saggin', braided hair
Suckers stare, but I don't care
My game ain't knowledge, my game's fear
I've no remorse, so squares beware
For my true mission is just revenge
You ain't my set—you ain't my friend
Wear the wrong color your life could end
Homicide's my favorite binge.

Colors

The police said that such measures were necessary to assure the children's safety.

The parents and teachers rejected the plan, but not because they thought it was too expensive or too drastic. Instead they said that trying to protect the children only on the school grounds was not enough, because the streets in front of the school would continue to be dangerous. They also wanted safer streets, but the police could not promise to make the streets safer.

So the parents decided to try something else. They decided to try to improve the neighborhood. Because drugs were bought and sold right in front of the school, the parents realized that their battle for a safer neighborhood was going to be a long one. But they are determined to try.

Although the wall around the elementary school in Oakland has never been built, a man and woman in Boston built a very different kind of wall.

The Boston Memorial

John and Dorcas Dunham own and operate Chez Vous, an inner-city roller skating rink frequented by gang members. The rink is located around the corner from one of the city's busiest police precincts. As many as 350 teenagers come in search of recreation each night. They are searched for weapons at the door.

John Dunham decided to make the names of young people killed by gang violence in Boston visible for his patrons to see. Just as the American government built a wall inscribed with the names of the Vietnam War dead as a memorial in Washington, D.C., Dunham built a wall and placed it in the back of the rink. It reads, "The Wall 1985-1990. Dedicated to Those Youth Who Died Before Their Time." On it, Dunham has inscribed the names of 65 teenagers who have died in recent years on Boston streets as a result of gang violence.

Dunham has the support of Audrey Moore. Her 11-year-old sister, Tiffany, is on the list. Tiffany was killed by a stray bullet one summer day when she was just sitting on a nearby mailbox.

"I talk to the gang members and try to get through," Moore says. "Maybe this will make them stop and think."

Dunham thinks it may do just that. He says he's seen fistfights stop suddenly when somebody calls the fighters' attention to the wall behind them.

"Some of the kids don't even come to skate anymore," Dunham said. "They're learning about respecting life, and that there are no second chances."

Street gangs are a major social problem in America. Walls to keep crime out of the schoolyard or to enshrine the names of murder victims do not begin to really solve the problem. What's called for is more involvement of people like David and Sister Falaka Fattah, Edwin and Rantine McKesson, and Michael Luckett.

David and Sister Falaka Fattah recently arrived in Portland, Oregon to open a halfway house for street gang members. The house will be a home to street youth seeking another way of life, and it will be similar to one the Fattahs have run for many years in Philadelphia.

In Detroit, Rantine McKesson and her husband Edwin are organizing neighborhood marches and boarding up local abandoned houses that might be used by drug dealers.

In California, a bingo parlor started by Michael Luckett is supporting the state's first privately-run crack clinic. Luckett started the bingo parlor because he was shocked to learn that five years after the crack craze hit the streets, there was still a long wait for anyone wanting to enroll in a treatment program. "People on the lower end of the socioeconomic ladder cannot wait for government to help with crack," Luckett says. "We will have to do it ourselves."

Fia Faletogo agrees. He is a Samoan social worker who works with the Sons of Samoa gang in Seattle. Faletogo began working with police and the Samoan community several years ago, taking Samoan kids to live with him until they could make it on their own without the gang. He has been credited with helping former members of the street gang find a better way of life.

Individuals can make a big difference, but they can't make all the difference. Community involvement is also necessary. There can be a dangerous side to community involvement, however, if people start taking the law into their own hands. Groups of people banding together to fight gang activity must be careful to work within the law. Might does not make right, whether that might is wielded by Bloods, policemen or concerned citizens.

Sergeant Bob Crawford, a 21-year veteran of the Oakland Police Department, has started enforcing housing codes against residents of drug houses. Since most drugs are sold in poor neighborhoods by drug dealers who live in rented houses, Crawford has used city laws to force drug dealers to move out of the hous-

Guardian Angels—recognizable in their white T-shirts and red berets—
are urban vigilantes who are anti-gang. They patrol many U.S. cities to protect
citizens from muggings and other acts of violence. The gang style of the
Guardian Angels has drawn criticism from law enforcement.

es and landlords to fix up the houses.

Because they do not live in these neighborhoods, some landlords will rent their houses to drug
dealers who are willing to pay high rent for the use of
a house where they expect to be left alone. Knowing
this, some Oakland organizations have sent busloads
of angry citizens to the doorsteps of absentee landlords
who live in other communities. Under pressure from

such groups, many absentee landlords have refused to rent houses to drug dealers.

Other groups in Oakland have persuaded the telephone company to install public phones that can only be used for outgoing calls. This prevents drug dealers and prostitutes from standing on the streets waiting for customers to call and arrange deals over the phone. It also frees up the phone for anyone wanting to make a call.

In Philadelphia, neighbors are getting together —if only to become more visible to gang members. "Unless the community comes up with ways to re-own the streets, the dealers will be back," says community organizer Peter Moor. "We want to get the barbecues going again."

Getting the barbecues going may be a good first step toward solving the problems of gangs and drugs in America. But it is only a first step, and a very local one at that. The gang problem is a big one. Any solution will only be as effective as the efforts made to resolve it.

Heroic individual efforts are helpful. Community involvement in the form of neighborhood associations is also necessary. And federal help in the form of dollars is essential. But some of the millions of dollars now being spent in the war on drugs might be better applied.

In addition to equipping federal drug agents with better means of protection, as is being done now, perhaps the federal government will consider investing in softball equipment, recreational centers, scholarships and job training programs. Making an effort to help young people stay away from crime is an investment in our future.

Glossary

BLOODS. A well-known Los Angeles gang, now spreading nationwide.

COLORS. The uniform of a gang member; the specific color of your shirt, bandana and/or shoes can indicate to others what gang you belong to.

COURTING-IN. The initiation of a new gang member, often accompanied by a beating from the gang itself.

CRACK. A form of the drug cocaine, mixed with other chemicals and processed into crystals. Smoking "rock" gets the user high in seconds.

CRIPS. A well-known gang, with groups or "sets" nationwide, that originated in Los Angeles.

HOMEBOY. A male friend or buddy, as in a fellow gang member.

ICE. A synthetic (laboratory made) drug that is highly addictive.

PROHIBITION. The era from 1919 to 1933 when it was illegal to manufacture, sell and consume alcoholic beverages. "Gangsters" were criminals who produced and sold liquor to millions of Americans during prohibition.

SKINHEADS. White males with shaven or nearly-shaven heads who form into gangs for the express purpose of harrassing people of other racial and ethnic backgrounds.

SETS. Rival members of the same gang; the Crips and Bloods have many "sets" that do not automatically get along.

TURF. A gang's territory, where they are the law—usually a neighborhood or urban district. Gangs often fight over turf, especially to control drug sales.

XENOPHOBIA. The fear of outsiders and people of different racial or ethnic backgrounds. In gangs, this usually applies to people from outside one's neighborhood or "turf."

Bibliography

Campbell, Anne. *The Girls in the Gang, A Report from New York*. Basil Blackwell Publisher Ltd., 1984

Moore, Joan W. *Homeboys: Gangs, Drugs and Prison in the Barrios of Los Angeles*. Temple University Press, 1972

Short, James F., Jr. and Fred L. Strodtbeck. *Group Process and Gang Delinquency*. The University of Chicago Press, 1965

Thrasher, Frederic M. *The Gang, A Study of 1,313 Gangs in Chicago*. The University of Chicago, 1936

Whyte, William Foote. *Street Corner Society: The Social Structure of an Italian Slum*. The University of Chicago Press, 1943

Yablonsky, Lewis. *The Violent Gang*. Penguin, 1970

Index

Picture Credits